the *Praying* in color journal

Sybil MacBeth

PARACLETE PRESS

BREWSTER, MASSACHUSETTS

The Praying in Color Journal

2008 First Printing

Copyright © 2008 by Sybil MacBeth

ISBN: 978-1-55725-618-8

Scripture quotations marked KJV are taken from the
Authorized King James Version of the Holy Bible.

10 9 8 7 6 5 4 3 2 1

Published by Paraclete Press
Brewster, Massachusetts
www.paracletepress.com

Printed in the United States of America

A message from Sybil MacBeth

When I first started *praying in color,* I couldn't stop. I was so excited to have a new way to pray for my friends and family. Prayer drawings littered my house. They showed up on all forms of paper— on backs of envelopes, on sketch pads, on shopping lists. No piece of paper was safe from my newfound prayer exercise.

Many of the prayers ended up in my journal next to my daily musings, reflections, and improvised poems. Since my journal was with me much of the time, so were my prayers. As a natural clutterer, I like the organization and safety of a journal. I can find my prayers. I can refer to old ones; I can add to them; I can pray the prayers again. The journal holds my prayer history and my ongoing efforts to pray unceasingly to the God who loves me unceasingly.

I hope this journal will provide you with a framework and safe deposit box for your *praying in color* prayers. The journal will also be your guide through the many different ways to pray described in *Praying in Color: Drawing a New Path to God.*

God's Peace Be with You,

Sybil MacBeth

Engage in an active, meditative, playful prayer practice.

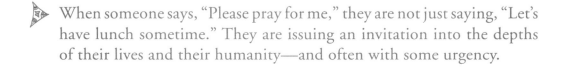

When someone says, "Please pray for me," they are not just saying, "Let's have lunch sometime." They are issuing an invitation into the depths of their lives and their humanity—and often with some urgency.

Praying for others is called *intercessory* prayer. When you offer intercessions you are asking God for a change of direction in the present course of someone else's life.

Make your prayer silent and wordless. There is no need to supply a pious or pleading monologue.

Look at the whole array of your loved ones on the page and know that, in spite of your fear and faltering words, you can hold them in prayer.

A clipboard, some paper, and a few markers turn any place into a prayer corner.

When your drawing is finished, you have a visual record of your prayers.

➤ When you move your focus from one person to the next, take a deep breath, recite a line from Scripture, or say, "Amen," or, "I'll be back."

Write your own name in a shape. Sometimes, the first person who needs prayers of intercession is you!

Think of this as kinesthetic improvisation, a kind of praying in tongues for the fingers.

Intercessory Prayers

 Each stroke and each moment is time that you spend with the person in prayer.

Choose random colors or choose colors that will stay in your memory, or remind you of the person for whom you pray.

Repeat the person's name to yourself as a way of corralling distracting thoughts. Think about the face or the entire person as if you were sitting with him or her in conversation.

Daydreams and distractions will probably enter your mind and demand center stage. If a thought returns more than once, write a single word on the page to remind you to address it later. If it's an obsessive thought, think of it as bathed in the colors of your prayers and not able to control you. If it's a task or chore that's calling you, write a one-word reminder so you can release it for future attention, but not forget it.

Linger with the page in front of you. Let the names, images, and colors imprint themselves on your heart.

Take this journal or page with you, if you can. Place it on your desk or refrigerator, or someplace where your eyes will rest on it during the day.

A flash of the image of your Prayer in Color during the day is a reminder that you have committed these persons to the care of God.

Remember, drawing is only half the prayer. The images on the page and in the mind are the visual alarm clock or Sanctus bells that remind us to pray.

The Scriptures are love letters

between God and God's people. They are about the promises and commitments between the God of salvation history and God's beloved human creatures. What do those promises and commitments have to say to you today?

An ancient Christian practice called *lectio divina*, or *divine reading*, is a way to bask in a word or phrase of Scripture and to let it transform us.

Lectio: Write the passage from Scripture. Allow the words to fill the page. Read the words slowly. Read the passage over and over again. Highlight or circle the word or phrase that speaks to you.

Meditatio: Write your chosen words on another page. Draw around or near the words. Let them be honored guests. Be patient and listen for the wisdom they deliver.

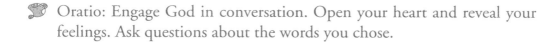 Oratio: Engage God in conversation. Open your heart and reveal your feelings. Ask questions about the words you chose.

Contemplatio: Let go of the words, thoughts, and feelings of the previous steps. Breathe evenly and enter into a quiet place. Climb into the imaginary arms of God and rest. If your body resists the stillness, draw with your eyes closed. Let the movement of the pen rock your mind into stillness and calm.

The possible ways to use this prayer practice

are as endless as your needs and your imagination.

Write all of the negative things you can think of on your prayer drawing. Don't hold back. God can take our garbage and turn it into compost.

We can be grateful and grumpy with a God in whom we trust. Listing your grievances one time and your thanksgivings another shows an effort to have an honest and intimate relationship.

Thanksgiving Prayers

Use your prayer drawings as a way to rehearse making amends or apologies with people. Doing this in person may or may not ever be possible, but the act of confessing on paper might result in unexpected resolution.

Chronicle the events of your spiritual journey in prayer drawings. Each step of your map-drawing will probably trigger other memories and help you see other ways your life has been infused with God's presence.

Pray for your mentors—the people who give you a new vision of yourself or the people who tell you the truth: a teacher who has kicked you off your complacent duff or a friend who tells you that you are acting like a turkey.

Mentors

Use words, drawing, and color to help verbalize and visualize who you are, whose you are, and what is important to you.

Consider praying about old wounds and hurts you are harboring.

Healing of Memories

Articulate—with words, drawing, and color—any old wounds in your life that need facing and resolution in your life.

Put as many names for God in your drawing as you can think of. What names speak to you?

Names for God

Names for God

 Let your drawings of the names of God become meditations on the ways you understand and expand your knowledge of God.

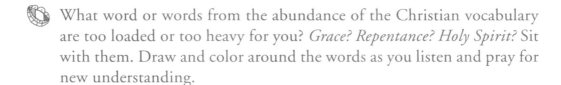

What word or words from the abundance of the Christian vocabulary are too loaded or too heavy for you? *Grace? Repentance? Holy Spirit?* Sit with them. Draw and color around the words as you listen and pray for new understanding.

Reflect on important concepts and ideas that have inspired you in books.

For Remembering

For Remembering

For Remembering

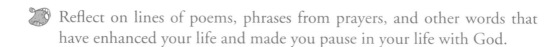

Reflect on lines of poems, phrases from prayers, and other words that
have enhanced your life and made you pause in your life with God.

For Discernment

Visualize the discernment and decision-making issues that you face. Release them as Prayers in Color.

For Discernment

 The process of drawing and writing can help you calm your worries.

During Advent or Lent, try to Pray in Color for different people, places, or situations (one each day) that are not part of your normal, everyday prayer life.

With Calendars

Create an intercessory calendar. Add a new person each day. Try this for a week or a month.

In Matthew's Gospel Jesus tells us, "Love your enemies, bless them that curse you, do good to them that hate you, and pray for them which despitefully use you, and persecute you" (5:44 KJV). Now, that's radical hospitality! We usually want to avoid our enemies, to forget that they exist. Even saying their names gives them a prestige we do not want them to have. Respond to Jesus' instructions by Praying in Color for someone you do not like.

For Your Enemies

For Your Enemies

This practice will probably not feel at all relaxing or playful. Writing the names of people you dislike or who dislike you can be a big step. When you are done, if you can stand it, hang the icon of your finished prayer in a prominent place. Whenever you see it, remember that person as a child of God.

About Paraclete Press

Who We Are

Paraclete Press is a publisher of books, recordings, and DVDs on Christian spirituality. Our publishing represents a full expression of Christian belief and practice—from Catholic to Evangelical, from Protestant to Orthodox.

We are the publishing arm of the Community of Jesus, an ecumenical monastic community in the Benedictine tradition. As such, we are uniquely positioned in the marketplace without connection to a large corporation and with informal relationships to many branches and denominations of faith.

What We Are Doing

Books

Paraclete Press publishes books that show the richness and depth of what it means to be Christian. Although Benedictine spirituality is at the heart of all that we do, we publish books that reflect the Christian experience across many cultures, time periods, and houses of worship.

We have several different series, including the best-selling Living Library, Paraclete Essentials, and Paraclete Giants series of classic texts in contemporary English; A Voice from the Monastery—men and women monastics writing about living a spiritual life today; award-winning literary faith fiction and poetry; and the Active Prayer Series that brings creativity and liveliness to any life of prayer.

Recordings

From Gregorian chant to contemporary American choral works, our music recordings celebrate sacred choral music through the centuries. Paraclete distributes the recordings of the internationally acclaimed choir Gloriæ Dei Cantores, praised for their "rapt and fathomless spiritual intensity" by *American Record Guide*, and the Gloriæ Dei Cantores Schola, which specializes in the study and performance of Gregorian chant. Paraclete is also the exclusive North American distributor of the recordings of the Monastic Choir of St. Peter's Abbey in Solesmes, France, long considered to be a leading authority on Gregorian chant.

DVDs

Our DVDs offer spiritual help, healing and biblical guidance for life issues: grief and loss, marriage, forgiveness, anger management, facing death, and spiritual formation.

Learn more about us at our Web site:
www.paracletepress.com
or call us toll-free at
1-800-451-5006.

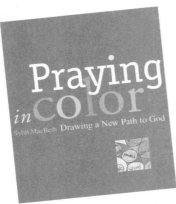

Also Available

Praying in Color

ISBN: 978-1-55725-512-9
$16.95, Paperback

Praying with the right side of your brain...

"This is the most invigorating and enabling book about prayer that I have seen in years! Wry, funny, accessible, wise beyond all appearances, and deeply spiritual, MacBeth warms the soul as well as the heart. So will praying in color."
–Phyllis Tickle, compiler, *The Divine Hours*

Use Praying in Color to help with:

- intercessory prayer
- lectio divina—reading the Bible for spiritual growth
- memorizing Scripture
- prayers for discernment
- creating a personal Advent or Lenten calendar
- praying for enemies

Praying in Color Workshop DVD

ISBN: 978-1-55725-549-5
$19.95, DVD

Everything you need to know to lead your own Praying in Color workshop, featuring author Sybil MacBeth.

Segments include:

- Arrival of participants and introduction to the practice
- Getting started
- Beginning to pray
- Bringing your prayer time to a close
